NO LONGER PROPERTY OF
ANYTHINK LIBRARIES /
RANGEVIEW LIBRARY DISTRICT

D1555915

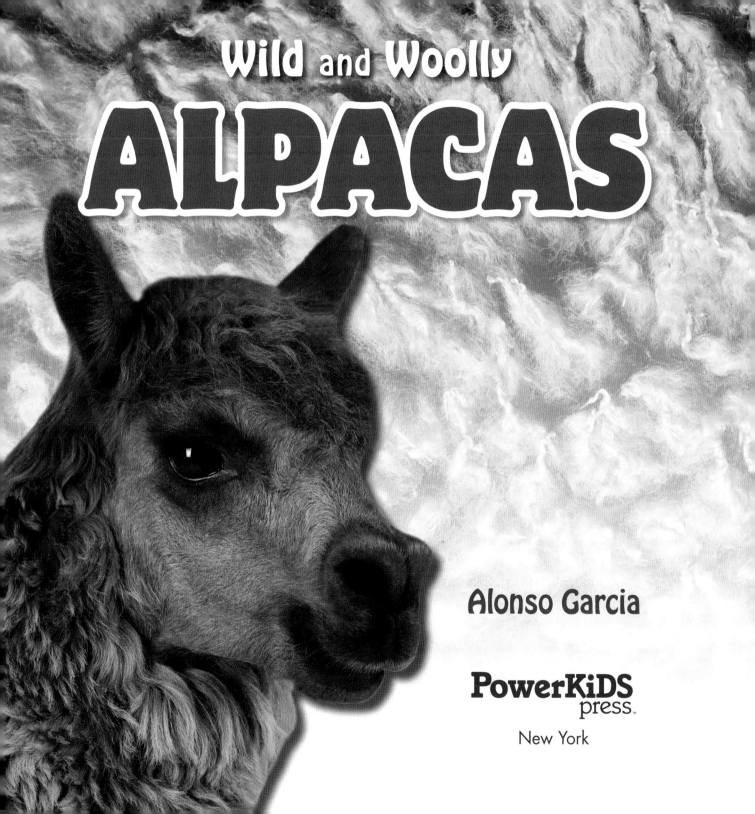

Wild and Woolly
ALPACAS

Alonso Garcia

PowerKiDS press.

New York

Published in 2018 by The Rosen Publishing Group, Inc.
29 East 21st Street, New York, NY 10010

Copyright © 2018 by The Rosen Publishing Group, Inc.

All rights reserved. No part of this book may be reproduced in any form without permission in writing from the publisher, except by a reviewer.

First Edition

Editor: Theresa Morlock
Book Design: Rachel Rising

Photo Credits: Cover, pp.1, 22 Eric Isselee/Shutterstock.com; Cover (background) Christian Heinrich/Getty Images; Back Cover, pp. 1, 3, 4, 6, 8, 10, 11, 12, 14, 16, 18, 20, 22, 23, 24 EcoPrint/Shutterstock.com; p. 5 (alpaca) pickypalla/Shutterstock.com; p. 5 (vicuña) Stefano Buttafoco/Shutterstock.com; p. 5 (llama) Harry Zimmerman/Shutterstock.com; p. 5 (guanaco) Palm Yutthana/Shutterstock.com; p. 7 jurb/Shutterstock.com; p. 9 sinagrafie/Shutterstock.com; p.10 Molly Marshall/Shutterstock.com; p. 11 Aunyaluck/Shutterstock.com; pp. 13, 15 Kira Volkov/Shutterstock.com; p. 14 iStockphoto.com/rgbdigital; p. 16 iStockphoto.com/Yarinca; p. 17 iStockphoto.com/Bartosz Hadyniak; p. 18 amadeustx/Shutterstock.com; p. 19 John & Lisa Merrill/The Image Bank/Getty Images; p. 20 astudio/Shutterstock.com; p. 21 Bob Hilscher/Shutterstock.com.

Library of Congress Cataloging-in-Publication Data

Names: Garcia, Alonso, author.
Title: Alpacas / Alonso Garcia.
Description: New York : PowerKids Press, [2018] | Series: Wild and woolly |
  Includes index.
Identifiers: LCCN 2017026250| ISBN 9781538325230 (library bound) | ISBN
  9781538325933 (paperback) | ISBN 9781538325940 (6 pack)
Subjects: LCSH: Alpaca-Juvenile literature.
Classification: LCC SF401.A4 G37 2018 | DDC 636.2/966-dc23
LC record available at https://lccn.loc.gov/2017026250

Manufactured in the United States of America

CPSIA Compliance Information: Batch #BW18PK: For Further Information contact Rosen Publishing, New York, New York at 1-800-237-9932

CONTENTS

What's an Alpaca?

With their long neck and weird body shape, alpacas look adorably odd. The sweet appearance of alpacas matches their gentle nature. But these animals are more than just cute. They're also very useful!

The relationship between people and alpacas began thousands of years ago in the region that's now Peru. The ancient people of South America **domesticated** alpacas to use them for their meat and fleece. Today, alpacas continue to be valuable livestock. Alpaca fleece is collected and made into soft, warm, sturdy **textiles**.

Alpacas are part of the Camelidae family. They're related to llamas, vicuñas, and guanacos. These animals look alike but have important differences.

alpaca

guanaco

vicuña

llama

5

Where Do They Live?

Today, alpacas can be found in many places around the world, but most live in Peru, Bolivia, and Chile. Their natural **habitat** is in the Andes Mountains of South America.

Alpacas **adapted** to survive in the harsh **environment** of the Andes. They have padded feet that allow them to walk on low-growing mountain grass without damaging it as they **graze**. Alpacas have a long neck, which helps them see predators from far away. Their long legs help them flee from predators.

Fuzzy Features

Alpacas' thick fleece keeps them warm and dry during the cold, wet winters in the Andes.

Some farmers keep alpacas as guard animals for sheep and chickens. Alpacas are tall enough to spot danger from a distance and can chase away foxes and dogs.

Alpaca Families

Alpacas live in groups called herds. Male alpacas are called *machos* and females are called *hembras*. A baby alpaca is called a *cria*.

Alpaca mothers are pregnant for about 11 months before they give birth to a *cria*, which can weigh from 12 to 20 pounds (5.4 to 9.1 kg).

Adult alpacas are about 3 feet (0.9 m) tall at the shoulder. They weigh between 100 and 175 pounds (45.4 and 79.4 kg). Alpacas can live for up to 20 years.

Fuzzy Features

Alpacas make a range of noises. They scream, snort, and hum. Watch out! Alpacas spit when they're upset.

When *crias* are old enough to eat solid food, they're called *tuis*.

9

Suri or Huacaya?

There are two breeds, or kinds, of alpacas: suri and huacaya (wah-KAY-uh). Suri alpacas have long hair that hangs straight down. Huacaya alpacas have fluffy fleece that sticks out.

suri alpaca

It's believed that Inca royalty wore fabrics made from suri fiber.

huacaya alpaca

Huacaya alpacas are much more common than suri alpacas. Of the millions of alpacas in the world, less than 10 percent are suris. As such, suri fleece and the fabric that's made from it are more highly valued. Suri hair is often used to make specialty and high-fashion textiles.

Fabulous Fleece

Alpacas come in about 20 different colors. They include white, black, brown, and many shades in between. The fiber has a sheen, or shiny appearance.

Alpaca fleece is soft and warm but also very strong. Unlike many other fibers, alpaca fiber is hollow, which allows it to hold in more heat. It's also water resistant.

Alpaca fiber is hypoallergenic, which means it's unlikely to cause an **allergic reaction**. That's because, unlike sheep wool, it has no lanolin. Lanolin is an oily matter.

Fuzzy Features

Fineness and crimp are two important qualities of alpaca fiber. Fineness refers to the thinness of the fiber, and crimp refers to its shape.

Farmers usually **shear** their alpacas during the spring so the animals don't overheat during the warmer months.

13

Shearing

Farmers shear alpacas once a year. It takes three people to shear an alpaca: a shearer to cut, a handler to hold the alpaca's head, and a third person to remove the fleece.

The alpaca is laid on a shearing table with its legs tied so it doesn't kick. Fleece from the back and belly is cut first because it's the most valuable. This is called blanket fleece. Fleece from the legs is often thrown away because it's too dirty to use.

← **shearing scissors**

Fuzzy Features

Each alpaca can produce 5 to 10 pounds (2.3 to 4.5 kg) of fleece. After the fleece is cleaned, it's sorted based on color, length, and quality.

Cleaning fleece by removing unwanted parts is called skirting. These unwanted parts may also be called skirtings.

15

Spinning

Spinning is the process by which raw alpaca fiber is made into yarn. Two processes used to prepare fiber for spinning are carding and combing. In carding, hand cards or drum cards are used to untangle and fluff the alpaca fibers. In combing, combs are used to pull all the alpaca fibers in the same direction.

Spinners are machines used to turn fiber into yarn. There are **mechanical** spinners and hand spinners. These tools stretch fibers and twist them together to form yarn.

← skeins

Fuzzy Features

Bundles of yarn are called skeins.

This photo shows a woman using a hand spinner to spin yarn. Spinning fiber takes a lot of skill and practice.

17

Dyeing

Once the fiber is spun into yarn, it can be dyed. Today, many people use synthetic dyes, which are made from artificial, or man-made, matter.

The people of the Andes Mountains traditionally used the region's rich resources to make natural dyes. Q'olle flowers are used to make shades of yellow and orange. Cochineal, a **pigment** produced by an insect, is used to create bright reds, pinks, and purples. The chilca plant is combined with a **mineral** compound called *collpa* to make green.

This woman is dyeing a skein of yarn by dipping it into a boiled dye mixture.

19

Weaving

Weaving is a process by which yarn is made into fabric. Weaving is usually done with a tool called a loom.

The loom **interlaces** pieces of yarn to create a tight-knit piece of fabric. Backstrap looms are simple machines made of wooden rods that have traditionally been used by weavers in the Andes. The weaver attaches herself to the loom and weaves the yarn together by hand.

Backstrap weaving requires patience and skill, but done correctly it can be used to make **intricate** patterns.

This Peruvian woman is weaving alpaca yarn on a backstrap loom.

21

Amazing Alpacas

People have kept alpacas for thousands of years. They spin and weave alpacas' thick, soft fleece into beautiful textiles. Alpacas are very useful livestock, and they're somewhat easy to keep. Alpaca fiber is one of the strongest natural fibers in the world. It's also warmer, softer, and more water-resistant than sheep's wool.

Alpaca fiber is so valuable that selling it can cover the cost of keeping them. It can last so long that alpaca textiles made 2,500 years ago have been found in Peru!

GLOSSARY

adapt: To change in order to live better in a certain environment.

allergic reaction: When a person's body responds badly to things in their surroundings that are usually harmless, such as dust, pollen, or insect stings.

domesticated: Bred and raised for use by people.

environment: The conditions that surround a living thing and affect the way it lives.

graze: To feed on grass.

habitat: The natural home for plants, animals, and other living things.

interlace: To wind or braid pieces together.

intricate: Having many parts.

mechanical: Having or using machinery.

mineral: A natural element that isn't a plant, animal, or other living thing.

pigment: A matter that gives things colors.

shear: To shave or cut fleece or wool off an animal.

textile: A kind of cloth that is woven or knit.

23

INDEX

WEBSITES

Due to the changing nature of Internet links, PowerKids Press has developed an online list of websites related to the subject of this book. This site is updated regularly. Please use this link to access the list: www.powerkidslinks.com/wandw/alpaca